MW00830865

To the girl called Life,

Thank you for helping me find my words all those years ago.

Note from the Author

I think that there is a certain power in the spoken word. When ink becomes so much more than just a thing on paper. *A Fools Guide to the Universe* was created with that in mind. This book is the collection of my conversations into the void over three years of the uncomfortable, tear-soaked moments with my thoughts & space.

Everything written here is meant to be spoken. To be screamed from the top of mountains when you find yourself hours away from home on a drive. Speak these words loudly, with friends, with family, with strangers, with yourself. Let these words be more than just symbols on paper. Feel them in every part of your body, just as they were felt in mine.

I am glad you are here. Be kind to yourself and everyone; we are all just floating through space, trying to find our way home.

sent with love from,

A fellow traveler.

i. Notes from the Universe

iii. Finding Home

i
Notes from the Universe

We may be thousands of miles away, but it is an honor to share the galaxy with you.

How Are You?

Do not tell me a lie.
How are you?
When was the last time you were able to look someone else
in the eye and speak the truth?
Are you riding high in the clouds of happiness
Or does it feel like every single day you are digging
yourself into a hole of uncertainty?
Are you fearful of what is coming later today?
Are you excited for the opportunity to say hey to someone
you haven't seen in years?
Will you allow their ears to hear the truth of how you feel?
Or will you seal your novel's worth of emotions behind a
six-letter phrase like we always seem to do?
"I'm good."

It has become our instant reply to a question we hear all too
often.
And that is when we learned to soften our voices,
To hide behind a curtain of "Not too bad" rather than open
the stage for "Not too good."
We never say what is going on.

And yet, we wonder why we are misunderstood.
When was the last time you spoke your truth?
When you grabbed what you are feeling by its roots,
and you opened up yourself to somebody else?
I know it's scary
To say the things you barely want to speak to yourself,
But truly.
How are you today?

A Friendly Reminder

That you
Have only ever seen yourself through photographs,
And the mirror.

You have never seen the way your smile beams
From its edges whenever you talk about something that you
love.
Or the way that your eyes light up at the sight of
Sunrises, coffee, or puppies!

So the next time someone tells you,
How beautiful you are.
Don't question it.
Because although you have never seen it—
Your beauty— I mean.

It is all that they know,
And they have been amazed by it
Every single day.

A letter to The Broken Hearted

To the ones, who's skin feels like a fiberglass hull adrift in an ocean of insecurity.
Breathe.
& allow your ballast tanks called lungs to fill you up & lift you from the bottom of the sea.
Remember, you are not an anchor dropped off to take the weight off of someone else's shoulders.
You, are a sail to be raised into the sky,
To ride through tsunami-sized waves!
You are an icebreaker carving your way through the Arctic Circle of recovery.
A miracle of strength,
Remember, you are not lost.
Merely, finding your way home
To a dock & a lighthouse,
Waiting to say hello.

Too Much

Love
With all your heart.
Love
As if Mozart decided to make his first piece of art
About them.
The first time I fell in love,
When it came to its end, she told me I was "Too Much."

Love
Is never "Too Much."
Love, Is like the hunch the Wright brothers had
About the beauty of the sky
It is every time the morning sun decides to rise
& why sometimes the clouds need to drop rain
Onto the soil
To remind the earth that sometimes,
it's okay to cry.

Love
Is never ashamed.
It is the never-ending flame
That some people will try to quench with change
But, no one ever asked the moon to change into the sun,
& No one ever told a spoon to bend itself into a knife
So don't let anyone ever take a slice of you
& try to mold it into something new.

Love
As if the winds had told you to.
As if God had hunched down from the sky, and
Turned down the music of doubt
Just so that you wouldn't miss out
When he told you there's no such thing

As loving someone too much.
Because love only tells the truth.
It is the restless, sleepless youth.
So love.
Love *too* much.
But first, love you
For all of your overflowing parts
Because sometimes the most beautiful art
Isn't the one on canvas
Sometimes it's the hands that made it.

Dear Mountains,

You make me feel small. But in a good way. The sheer magnitude of your cliffs & the way your trees reach for the sky reminds me that no force, even that of gravity, can stop your peaks from breaking through the clouds. I want to be like you. Never doubting your beauty, never ashamed of showing your most worn out & weathered stones. Never afraid of forces that tell you no. No part of you is perfect, but I am beginning to think that is the point. Every small piece of you, as battered, blooming, bruised & beautiful as they may be, are unique in every way they need.

Mountains, thank you for this small feeling. I will use it as a reminder that there is still a lot of room on this planet to dream bigger & thank you for reminding me to defy gravity. Nothing can hold me down, not even my own thoughts

Dear Mountains,
Thank you

A message to the Sun Chasers:

better known as the dreamers, aka the crazies, sometimes called the naive. The ones who have big dreams & even bigger hearts. The world will try to limit your spirit, to force your ideas back into your dreams, and tell you that what you feel isn't "practical" or "can't be done." Do not allow them. Do not limit your goals & ambitions to your dreams. We are all, at a time, dream chasers. But at some point, we must become Sun Chasers instead. To take our dreams into the light and make them a reality, to chase after the things that not only sit in our minds but in our hearts as well. That new job, new location. To finish the canvas sitting in your closet, to write that book. Our lives should never be limited to the confines of our dreams but rather made limitless by the endless possibilities of what could be. To the Sun chasers.

Dream big, but chase bigger.

Sailors

Give me the **rain**.
Give me the **wind**.
Give me the way the **sun** beams from the seams of the sky.

Give me the orchestra of **birds** from outside my window on
the days that I stay home.
Give me the feeling of the **ocean** & the embrace of **fellow
sailors** in these turbulent seas.
Give me the **succulents** & the joy they gleam, even when
stuck in small spaces.

Give me every part of this **world** & how it amazes me.
Right now, I may be distant,
But I can't wait to find out what more there is to see.

Break Me Down

You may break me down.
Break me down into little pieces until I don't know who I am.
Break me down into little pieces, so I may fit inside of a box.
Break me down from the top of my existence to the bottom of my soul.
You may break me down until I can't see the pieces of what I thought I use to be.

But please,
Break me down with step-by-step written instructions of how to put myself back together again whenever I am ready.
You see, I've been broken down so many times that the ground and I have become really close friends.

However,
You may break me down multiple times, but I will get back up numerous times more.
I will kindle a friendship with the sky despite the multiple times I have fallen from its reach.
You may break me down so far that for a time, I won't be able to recognize myself in the mirror,
but I will always be there to build myself back up.
You see, I am a sand dune that can move with the wind but can't be destroyed by even our most powerful weapons on earth.
Like bullets and word.
You see, I am a sound too loud
To ever stay broken down.

Long Way Home:

I hope they choose to take the long way home.
Just so it doesn't feel like you are just another thing taking
up an ounce of their time
Because they want to give gallons to you.

I hope they help you slow down your walk.
I hope they remind you that the destination will always be
there.
But right now,
We are here.

I hope that when your hands shake
They help you make music from the strums.

That when you can't seem to find the words inside of your
lungs,
They will sit next to you & let you feel whatever you need.

I hope they choose to love you like the soil loves the trees,
Enough to give you all the space you need.

17

A Fool's Guide to the Universe: lesson #19

Worth

You are never too difficult to love. Remember, our planets circle around a flaming ball of gas, not because it's easy, but because it's worth it.

Long Live the Artist.

The wanderer,
The storyteller,
The daring & cunning.

The souls of enchanted faith to create.
To weave air into existence & sow the path between heart
& mind.
The ones whose eyes light up at the signs of sunsets &
sunrises.
Whose minds race with the sound of wind through
mountains.

Long live the artist.

Little Star

Little star,
You are far away in a section of the universe that you may
not know.
But you are not alone.
We are all little stars in our own unknown orbits

They say that you can't make a sound in space.
But I hope you can hear us chanting you on from far away
in our own little sections of the universe
Little star stay true.
We will see you soon

Human

And the Statue of liberty said,
"Give me your tired, your poor, your broken, huddled
masses yearning for something more."
She spoke like a poet,
Begging for each curve of all your edges.
Each mosaic of humanity,
With hands outstretched to embrace each fabric of you.

Do not go quietly.

Go loud.
Go.
Like the orchestra that has practiced for years,
Just ready to be heard.

You
Are this beautiful mosaic of mix-matched history, of love,
& galaxies worth of stories.
So burn bright.
Show off the edges of your human,
Like the stories we are all so excited to hear
Like the sound of the first terrifying step out of bed.

Go into this,
Into this life.
Take it by its clothespins
Wear it like the superhero capes of our childhood.

You are needed here more than ever.

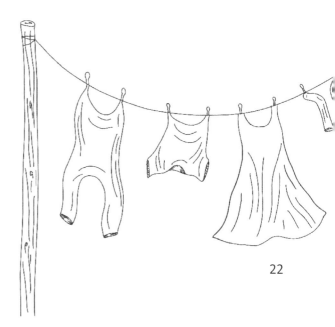

A Fool's Guide to the Universe.
Lesson #4

Anger

Yell from rooftops when the world tries to crumble you.
We have light-years of space open for your voice to be
heard, scream loud, and let the world ring out.

✳ **Celebration**

Here is to getting up at 6 A.M.
Or whenever you feel like it.
To good hair days
& old cliches.
To midnight coffee breaks.
To cake...or pie if that's what you're into.

Here is to sunrises and sunsets.
To new music.
To box sets of Harry Potter.
Here is to the last otter you saw at the zoo
& here is to the hope that he will be set free soon.
Here, is to the sun at noon to wake you up after a long night
out with friends.
To friends who still invite you places when you said you
were okay staying home
To true friends who come home to check on you when you
are not okay.

Here is to the days that you feel beautiful
& even the days that you don't.
Because you are never one to boast
But I will be damned if we don't talk about how good you
look in that coat.

After 21 rotations.

My advice is simple.

Take deep breathes.
Smile as often as you can, even when it hurts
Remember,

You have so much more to give,
so keep giving.

My Son

For when the time comes

I want to be able to tell my son a story about how **we found world peace.**
I want to tell him a story about our fight for equality.
I want to make sure his first instinct isn't to run.
I want him to go to a school where he **never has to fear a gun**.

I want him to live in a society where the concept of **love** is what holds them together rather than tears them apart.
I want him to see the world as a **piece of art**.
I want him to see the Amazon Rainforest and be amazed by the greens and blues,
And how the rain continues to persist.
I want him to live in a world where the Amazon still **exists.**

I want him to **love who he loves** because love is where we begin.
I even want him to love the people who choose to hate him just because of the **color of his skin**.
I want him to know that his body was a gift given to him by the earth so he could experience it all.
And I hope he gets to see sunsets, and sunrises that will always leave him in awe.
You see, I want to teach him to listen to people's beliefs with open ears
I hope years from now he is able to swim with the coral reefs.

You see, I hope.
That he will get to live a life with world peace.
I hope,
That he will do whatever it takes to fight for equality
I hope
He will never have to make up for our mistakes.

Do you hear that?

Listen, do you hear that?
It's a voice from across the room that says that you
Don't belong here
Listen, do you hear that?
It's the echo from the back of your mind that says that you
Aren't beautiful.
Listen, do you hear that?
It's the sounds of a teacher's pen striking paper that says that you
Aren't smart enough.
Listen, do you hear that?

It's the breaking of heartstrings the moment they say that they,
Don't love you anymore.
Trust me,
I know some days this life can feel like a record store full of
broken albums of soundtracks that we shouldn't even be listening
to.
Like rap music in grade school.
But, I promise you that somewhere between these stacks of
absurdities
Lies the soundtrack of hope.
When I was 12 years old, I learned that music can help me cope.

I allowed my headphones to become earplugs
And let the music give me a hug in place of the friends that didn't
exist.
As I got older, I learned that everyone has music inside of their
souls.
But I suppose some of us got used to the silence.
We drowned out the noise until we Were Unable to hear the
music being sung to us, even by people who actually care.

Hurtling

Tell me
how boring can our life actually be
when we are hurtling through space
with no destination.
Just hope that we never crash.

Gardens and Cemeteries

When I was a kid, I was told that the only thing
That separates a cemetery & a garden
Is what you choose to put in the ground

So when my mind runs around on days like this,
I choose to bury my past,
Cremate my insecurities,
& spread them into mist.
You see, I often dive deep into my soul
In search of my gold
My beautiful fertilizer of existence.
I am persistent in the belief that you
Are not some weed to be plucked from the ground
& chucked around, like grandmothers' ashes
Between feuding relatives.
You are the superlative of what it means to be alive.
You are the reason why every hummingbird decides she
needs to fly.
Why every honeybee would give his life for the simple
pollen of your laughter.

You are not the aftermath of someone else's weed-
whacking.
You are the resounding clapping of angels when the first
sunflower decides to bloom in the spring.

You ring out like church bells being lifted
Into the sky by roses outside
Of the last cemetery of doubt.
They may call you nothing more but daisies to be thrown
out,
But never forget to stand proud
With your thorns out!

Reaching to be lifted up by the sky & this is for the dimes
you gave away,
Trying to buy yourself flowers
When it feels like hours and hours of time
Go by with nothing more than rain showers.
But never forget that after every drop
Of rain comes down,
your garden
will stand proud.

A Fool's Guide to the Universe: Lesson #27

Gravity

Is not based on size. There are neutron stars a mere mile wide that dwarf the sheer magnitude of stars 10,000x their size. Little star, you may be small, but our universe is large. & Your arms reach farther than you believe.

A Note from Space:

Let's make like stars.
Even when everything around us says otherwise.
Let our light be like music & send echoes through this
place.
Even long after we are gone.
Let's make like the stars.
Creating a home here together,
A perfect mosaic of
Interconnected constellations.

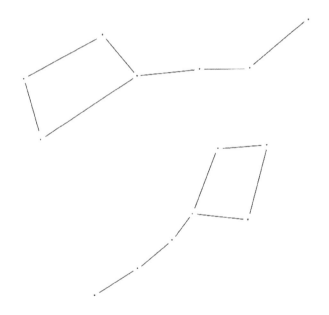

Bend

When the weight of the world feels heavy.
Remember,
That your shoulders have held up galaxies.
That your eyes tell stories that some people may never
believe
& your heart, as battered and bruised as it may be,
Has crossed oceans just to get you here.

Your body,
Your soul,
You.

Were made to bend but not break.
To sway in the wind but never fall.
& when the rest of the world seems to be falling at its
edges,
We will still be here.
Together, I mean.
Adrift in this galaxy we call home.

I am excited to hear the stories that your eyes tell.

Return

Give me questions.
I will return with answers.
Give me uncertainty.
I will return with clarity.
Give me doubt.
I will return with proof.
Give me fear,
& I will return to you with hope.

ii

When Floating

Even in this massive place, we were bound to cross paths.

Love like stars

I hope that someone chooses to love you with the same
commitment as stars.
Even when surrounded by darkness,
Choosing to shine as bright as they can to light up the night
sky for you.

May I

May I never become so rich that I forget the grass.
May I never become so proud that I forget to ask, please
May I never become so loud that I forget to breathe.

You see, may I never allow myself to forget where I come
from.
That place where the ground and sky break when the
mountains move towards the horizon.

Please.

May I never be so consumed about who I can be that I
forget who I am.

I was born on the coast, where music rises from the waves,
and you can hear the mist sing to you.

Please.

May I never forget this

Reply

The voice in the back of your mind whispers,
"You aren't beautiful."
& You reply,
"Beauty is in the eye of the beholder."

So it laughs and says,
"You are made up of mistakes & flaws."
You smile and reply,
"There are no such things as mistakes, just happy
accidents" & I have been drawing outside of the lines for
years.

It sneers and yells,
"They will never love you!"
You nod,
"so then maybe I'll just have to love myself."

It burns and cries,
"You are an awful person!"
You sigh…
"No, I am a good person who may have done awful
things."

Filled with anger, it screams,
Who do you think you are?!
Fearlessly you reply,
I am me, & you no longer control the things that I do.

The voice leaves for a time.

Let me remind you,
You are not a one-sided story.
You are not alone.

When the edges of your human feel so battered & bruised,
When the voice's noose-shaped dialogue feels like it is
crawling up from the ground in which you buried it.
We will bring the farthest reaches of the sky to you.
Like the orchestra that outshines the cemetery doubt,
Every morning you find yourself questioning the mirror.

My dear, your voice, your shape, your demeanor
Is a beautiful mosaic of art
That no matter of darkness can take away from you.
Do not give them that power.

Dear soldier, you are not alone.
Every second, minute, hour,
We will stand by you.
Give in to every piece of human that you are.
Every misstep, every perfection, every curve & every
edge.
Let this moment serve as the reminder that you are not
alone.
For every village was made by people & we are here to
welcome you home.

Baby Steps

While our universe was made in an instant,
It is said that it took millions of years to bring us into
existence.
While life moves so fast,
You don't have to.
My friend, take some days in baby steps,
Look around & admire the beauty that surrounds you.
Laugh at the fact that you are 13.8 billion years in the
making
& love like you have 13.8 billion more to learn every
aspect of the one you adore.
Slowly, but always sure to be moving forward.
No matter how many steps it takes.

Dear Anxiety:

Remember,
That if you try to convince my hands to shake like
tambourine drum sets,

I will make music with them.

If you try to convince my skin to crawl away from my
body,

I will stay here, ready to welcome it back in

& if you try to trick my lungs into forgetting their function,

I will stand tall, chest out.
Ready to breathe this air in that you have worked so
hard to keep me from.

This life
That I am ready to live.

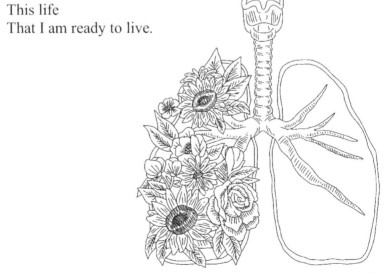

Cliff

Here's to the things you can and cannot do.
To the things we try but are told cannot be true.
The things that make us and break us.
The I love you's to the I can'ts.
To the at 3 A.M. dance in the morning when all stops
making sense
Here
is to the things that don't make sense.
Like Dreams.

Here's the cliff that keeps everything from being new.
The single inch that keeps me and you from doing the
things that we know we should do.

Here
is to what hope brings.
Because on one side, you have a cliff that leads you to the
unknown or what the future could hold
& the other side you have safety from the things that you
don't know could be true.
Because maybe they are waiting for you
To decide what you can and cannot do.

Desert Dreams.

I will be here fighting this dream as stubborn as sand.
You may move me,
Toss me to the wind.
I may land thousands of miles away,

But I will never give up on this dream.

A Fool's Guide to the Universe.
Lesson #16

Attention

Take time to connect the dots of the constellations in people's eyes. How easy it is to be lost in those who get lost in you.

Iterations

I hope you find someone
who loves your endless versions.
Your multiple iterations.
The indescribable translations of the parts of you that you
are still figuring out.
Someone, as dedicated as an Apple consumer willing to
camp outside of stores in the dead of winter.
Just for the chance to see you
In your newest form.
I hope you find someone
Who will bear every storm.

Planets: You

I think the most amazing thing about life is
That no matter how hard we try,
We will never be in the same place twice.
Not even in our own homes.
Because just like Pluto, Earth & Mars,
We are all planets racing around
Our one singular star.
In constant states of change
In which our definitions of love & life
Become new every single day.

I say this why?
Because maybe sometimes
Our ideas of love
Just have not found our orbits yet.
Maybe, the pathway you were meant to take
Has not become a constellation within your sky tonight.

But just like every 365 days,
The planets that we call bodies—
Our earth,
Our life—
Finds its way around our one singular star.
Maybe this is only the start
For you.
Because in an entire universe full of art
Maybe you
Can be the start.

Like Water

I don't know when love will come.
But I hope it comes to you like water.
I hope it flows into every part of you.
Even some of the places that you didn't even know existed.

I hope it helps you build a garden.
Inside of yourself to bloom like the flowers and trees
That you hold in your hands.

I hope it helps you breathe new life into the soil
That you have cared so deeply for.

Falling.

At this point in my life,
I have been skydiving 3 times,
& now I have realized that the feeling of hurtling yourself
towards the earth—
Only trusting the person on your back to hold you—
As you race towards the ground.

Is a lot like love.

I guess that's why they also call it **falling**.

# Discount

Can I please get a discount on courage?
& why can't I find confidence on the clearance rack?
Can anyone please explain to me why it feels like my soul
purchased anxiety in bulk?
You see, I was told that strength is found within ourselves,
so why do my shelves feel so empty all the way down aisle
3 right in between the future and poetry?

Listen, I get that sometimes this galaxy-sized grocery store
may run out of inventory of the things that I may need more
of than the average customer.
Like notebook paper, coffee, or bravery.
But it would really help
If it could keep a few things on hold for me.
Like love, courage… and maybe some more coffee!
Because I will never accept the 99 Cent Store versions of
those 3 things
Because I will never, *ever* accept 99% of certainty… or
caffeine for that matter!

Listen, I don't have much.
But I do have this.
It is a spirit, battered & bruised over history that doesn't
deserve an encore,
But hopefully before this is all over, I'll have enough to buy
this whole store.
& layout courage like it is a yard sale & the final price is a
smile.
Hang up empathy like it is a flyer for 100% off bottles of
kindness,
And maybe even leave myself a gift card to courage
Because sometimes that might be the hardest thing to find.

A Fool's Guide to the Universe: Lesson #14

Limitless

The only thing faster than the speed of light is the amount of time it takes to love someone.

To the voice who saved me.

The one with outstretched arms that reached down into my
darkest parts.
The one who turned my most battered and bruised pieces
into art so beautiful even Michelangelo would gawk at.
The one who was able to withstand heartbreak, anxiety &
depression just long enough for me to understand what it
means to be alive.
The one who knew, gradually, with time, I would be able to
realize that I am not some piece of broken rubble waiting to
be thrown out by the latest excavator searching for love.
So, to the voice who saved me.
Thank you.
But my friend, I'm sorry.
I guess I never expected that you
would sound a lot like me.

Noctum

How lucky we are to be in the presence of stars.
For the night sky is shared through your eyes.
And I could stay here till dawn.

Rough Parts

Give me the things that I need more often than the things I want.
You see, I hope the universe brings us to our knees every time we start begging for the sun more often than we are thankful for the rain.
I never want to know love without heartbreak.
I want the universe to take me for my best parts...and my worst ones.
Just as I try to take people for theirs.
We are not perfect.
But I hope we never try to.
Scientists say that for giant redwood trees to grow, they must first burn at over 1000 degrees until they gain the courage to release their seeds back down to the earth.
This.
This is for the people still burning.
The rooftop dreamers,
The naive believers,
The late-night shower singers.
You see, this is for the people with rough parts.
With sandpaper in their history.
The out of tune orchestra performers,
The two left feet dance club-goers,
The poets still finding out how to rhyme.
You don't need to hide.
You need to let your rain shine.
And yes, I said *RAINshine* as in,
Let your best and worst parts be on display
Because you are not just your name.
Not just your biggest mistake or your shiniest trophy.
You,
Are the perfect story

Built-up of highs & lows,
Lessons learned and lessons earned,
& this is for you.
Lean on it.
When all else fails,
Let it remind you that you are the masterpiece of
everything we call art.
You are a hot thunderstorm,
A bright shadow,
A cold volcano.
You are every part you.

✳ Short Documentary.

I wish the first person I ever fell in love with was myself,
That I could look inside of the mirror & see the person that
I always dreamed of.
But I am still getting there.

There are some days that this body
Feels as if it doesn't belong to me.
Like I am an actor playing inside of a role that was
somehow given to me,
But I know at some point I will have to take control
& become the director.
I will be the person in charge of my own destiny.
That I am worth every piece of this.
That I belong to all of it.

But I know
It will come slowly.
This is not a short documentary.
This is a feature film
& we're only in the first act.

Note From a Coffeeshop:

When the world feels like too much.
When the weight of the universe finds its way onto your
shoulders.
When your eyes feel heavy with time.
Come into this.
We made you a cup of coffee (or tea).
Don't worry, we know how you like it.
You are safe here.
You don't have to steer this ship alone.
We are all sailors just finding our way home.
But right now,
The world is quiet & the universe can wait.
So open your eyes.
Cheers.

Keys.

You remind me of piano keys.
You walk into a room with a thunderous sound,
But your heart speaks subtle melodies.
You can pause a room & bring them to applause—your
musician's heart.
Never let them quiet you.

Missteps

I am a collection of missteps,
Of shades outside of the lines.
Autocorrect fixes and missteps.

I used to carry an eraser in my pocket.
Now I just leave my brushstrokes and hope someone calls it
art.

Hurricane

I heard once that *wind*
was just the earth's way of making music.
I never thought I would wish to hear a hurricane

Time-stop

Look for the moment when time stops
When the crickets hush,
The wind calms,
The ocean relaxes its hold on the sand.
There you will find me

    The peace in the quiet
    The music in the darkness

iii

Finding home.

Universe, Virgo supercluster, Local Group, Orion's Arm, Sol System, Earth,

Home.

Let down your heavy shoulders,
Relax your jaw,
Take that breathe.

You are safe now.

✳ Roam

My bones ask for the ocean,
& my heart longs for the mountains.
My skin wishes to feel the summer sun,
& my feet beg to run through open fields.
My nose, it requests to smell fresh pine cones,
While my hands itch for the feeling of snow.
My lungs dream of air locked away in caves.
My tastebuds write about coffee from hidden cafes.
My mind desires to be set free in the sea.

You see, every part of me needs to be free.
To travel & explore
To get lost & roam
To make every place feel like **home.**

& yes.

There will be winters.
But, there will also be springs & summers
Where the anxiety doesn't feel like it rattles your bones.
When you don't shiver & shake at the idea of just getting out of
bed.

& yes.
There will be falls.
When it feels like all the work has come to an end.

But just remember,
That spring will always come
& this winter too shall pass.

Cats & Dimes

I always have to keep my change.
So, to Coffee shop baristas with open minds, I'm sorry
But, these dimes are mine.
You see, I have this bag of change & it reminds me of you.
It hangs on the passenger side across from the glove
compartment
So that every time I drive down roads without you by my
side,
I can try to reach in and grab dimes that will hopefully
bring up parts of your spine.
Because sometimes,
These roads seem to be a lot more lonely when stars seem
to interact as places
We never seem to be at.

& these dimes, pennies, and quarters begin to feel like
shoulders,
Worn heavy like well-traveled roads
Going blind like bats down these deserted streets,
Looking for these cats that have nickels on their collars
That rattle like the echoes of your name.

Because sometimes this bag of change,
Becomes music inside of its rattling cages.
Because sometimes I try to remember.
Because I always seem to forget
The sound of your voice
During times like this.

& As if God had somehow replaced your vague memory
with
A streetlamp, a desert road & a family of cats.
I now seem to scratch at the memory of you.
Like a blind man on his knees in search of brail.
I scale down to the earth, searching for these pennies,
nickels, quarters, and dimes
Because they flood back memories that were the chimes of
your voice.

You see, when I was a kid, I was told
The only thing that separates a cemetery and a garden is
what you choose to put in the ground.
So, I started pounding these dimes down, down, down until
I saw a crown of sunflowers rise up out of the ground to
remind me of the scent of your hair
When we sat together under streetlamps looking for your
little family of cats.

Music

I don't know much about love.
But I do know this.
Music is felt in your heart
before it is heard in your ears.

So, I hope you find your favorite tune.
A song that doesn't have to be loud,
For you to know it's true.

A Fool's Guide to the Universe: lesson #13

Luck

People who have never met someone who makes them feel alive simply because of how they smile will call it luck. Others will call it fate.

Amor Fati

The words *Amor Fati*

Mean "the love of fate."
I hate the idea that we have given up on hope.
That we needed an idea.

Love is a set of conscious & unconscious thoughts.
Like how we breathe.
We do it naturally, but there are times that we need to stop
And take a deep breath.
So, we force our bodies to give up all of their boundaries
And say, "I am going to do this right now."

I think love is the same way.
A conscious idea, a conscious decision
to do the thing we do naturally,
but this time with a little more emphasis

Searching.

I refuse to view my body as too broken
simply for the fact that we actively search for craters on
other
planets

just to get to know them.

Things I am still learning

There are a few things that I am learning,
slowly.
The first being
That this body is not a punching bag hanging from events
that were outside of my control.
That this soul is a home too expensive for the impoverished
ideals of someone else's expectation.
That while I have this purple heart from being battered &
bruised by my own misunderstanding of a four-letter word,
It is not taken lightly.
Deem absurd
Or treated like a warzone on the brink of escalation by
people who were never trained in the special forces
operation of handling someone with care.
Slowly, I understand that the air inside of my lungs has no
mute button.
So, when I raise my hands in dispute over the mistreatment
of my jumbled mess of poorly worded metaphors, coffee &
bones,
It is because I have found a home in the reconciliation of
what it means just
To be
Me.

A beautiful mess.
God's unruly second best.
You see, I was born feet first
& from that point on, my mother could've sworn that the
most jagged parts of me would always find their rhythm

Because I am not the symptoms on Wikipedia's absurd
definition of anxiety, depression, and mania.
No.
I am the universe's incredible obstruction.
It's a resounding deduction of what it means to be alive.
Its beautiful introduction of the dimes and pennies I gave to
the sky
On the many, lonely, nights I thought it was over.
You see this
Is not over.
Is only the beginning of what it means to be living.
Slowly, I am beginning to understand
That no matter what.
No matter when
Negativity decides to send you its most battered pieces,
You must stand proud.
Hammered into the ground so much that no universal force
could push you down.
Slowly,
I am beginning to understand
What it means to be me again.

Dear storyteller:

Do it—scared.
Burn at both ends & write your story in constellations.
It will feel strange, like you don't belong where you are,
Like your voice is too small for the space it is trying to fill.

But my dear,
Share & share boldly.
You are a galaxy's worth of stories
that we are all so excited to hear.

Shooting stars

I like to believe that parts of all shooting stars
end up in our eyes when we sleep.
I see the galaxies in yours as proof.

The Young, Wild & Creative

Remember, my dear friends, you are the Young, the Wild & the Creative. Never let anyone convince you otherwise. You see, youth is a mentality. I have met 80-year-olds with such joy that they are 17 and 17-year-olds with such little faith that they are 80. The world will try to make you grow up too fast but take every day on with the spirit of a child, joyous, and new.

You are wild; never let them tame your spirit. Society will ask you "to be more practical," to dream less, & hush your voice, but you are wild. Live loud & sing the anthem of your existence on your highest setting.

You are creative. In whichever way you choose. Never let them tell you otherwise

Airplanes and Highways

I always have to have a window seat.
Some days, because I just want to beat the rush in the case
of an emergency exit
But others,
Because I get to see the highways,
& They remind me of where I've been.
You see, as someone with a traveling heart you know all
too often
What it's like to be up in the sky.
Lost,

With outstretched arms like 747's
In search of the next airport.
The next place with enough concrete foundation
To make your unstable engines feel safe enough to land
Without a standing ovation from surrounding passengers
But, who's ever heard of a smooth landing?

Sometimes my stamped out heart feels like the torn pages
of passports,
Finding themselves crashing down onto freeways
Like paper planes getting lost to the wind by grade-
schoolers
I often have to remind myself that some turbulence
does not require a new life insurance policy
Due to an emergency landing on the 405.
But sometimes, it just means they need a little extra fuel
And a readjustment, of course.
From Dallas to Rome,
In search of that one airport
Who're arms
Feel like home.

A Fool's Guide to the Universe.
Lesson #7

 *Courage*

It took the earth a lot to ask the moon to dance. But they have waltzed around the planets for years.

Scars

When I was 8 years old,
I fell off my bike & landed face first.
I earned this little mark on the right side of my eyebrow.
I often think of the little scars we carry around—
From heartbreaks, mistakes
Laughs, sighs
High fives & goodbyes.

You see, I was once asked how I got all these scars.
I laughed and told them
I got this one from the first time I gave my heart to
someone who didn't deserve it.
This one from an argument that got a little too physical.
This one from the time my mind got a little too mystical &
I thought I could fly.
And I got this one from the time I had to remind myself
that my scars are what make me beautiful,
Not just something unsuitable to someone's interpretation
of perfection.

You see, my scars
Are not some bars that keep me from the next portion of
my history.
They are the clues that unravel the mystery of the thing that
we call "Life."
And I am taking the marks & turning them into art.
Taking these wounds & turning them into the route I take
along this yellow brick road home
Because I am a mosaic of lessons learned & lessons
earned.
And I will continue. To always
Be a work in progress.

Galaxies.

My dear, I see the series of Galaxies running loose through
your eyes.
Like the connect the dot paintings that make constellations.

I am glad we're here,
In this galaxy, I mean.
Like the dance of the sun and the moon,
May these days never end.

Dreamer Point North

Dreamer, point north
Like a lighthouse,
Aim your beam to wherever your dreams happen to be.
Play the strings inside of your heart so loud that nothing
could pick apart the absolute masterpiece of art that is your
existence.
Dreamer, They will try to stop you.
The neighbors will file a noise complaint about how the
concert of ambition going on inside your brain echoes
throughout the house.

But listen to the sound of your soul drawing you into the
ocean.
Because while it is scary that there are no paved roads on
your path, trust in that fact that dreams
Don't always come with a map.
No matter how deep the water around you may seem at the
time,
My dear dreamer, point north.
Look up into the sky and allow the stars to guide you
no matter what tries to change your course,
Dreamers always point north.

Resume

Hi, My name is Donovan.
I am a writer, photographer, filmmaker, artist & general human being
& that's really hard to write on a resume.
I am still learning to say that some days I am not okay.
I have a fear of heights, but I have jumped out of planes.
I make things that can last forever, but I never seem to be able to make people stay for longer than a few days.

I am really good at emotions, but really bad at explaining the things that I feel.
I write about courage but run for the hills every time the girl of my dreams walks into the room.
I am a walking contradiction still unable to make the distinction between night and day
& those are all hard things to put on a resume,
But here you go.

Hi, My name is Donovan Alexander Beck
I'm 5 foot 5… and a half.
My skills include writing poetry, taking photos, and crying
for absolutely no reason.
My nationality is human.
I believe that music is the key to the soul.
My home is wherever coffee is found.
My references are my local barista and Instagram
& my education is from the University of Youtube.
I don't know much,
But I do know this.
My one goal in life is to leave this earth better than how I
found it.
& I am proud enough to write that anywhere.
Even here.
So I may be a walking contradiction—
An insane inscription on today's history—
Still trying to figure out this mystery that we call life.
But I think that I am happy enough to say,
That it will all be okay.

Acknowledgments

Thank you to my family. My Parents, Frederick & Christine, my siblings, Jasmine and Jaquari. The words found here were crafted in the space and faith you instilled in me.

Thank you to my creative family, Caden, Hayden, Nou, Zoe, Nathan, Sarah, Emily and so many more. You make me strive to be the artist I am every day.

Thank you to Houston, Jesse, John, Tara and my community at HaitiPartners & GoodWork. You taught me that the community is the most valuable resource we have.

Thank you to Lauren. My illustrator, biggest advocate, and best friend. These pages would be nothing without you.

To my teachers and mentors at CADA, Ron, Jeff and so many more. You remind me every day that supporting the next generation of creatives and world changers is my most important mission

To Scott, Emma, and Mackenzie. Thank you for looking at this book with your beautifully objective minds and saving me in the scary world of proper grammatics & punctuation.

To the girl called *Life*. Thank you. Know that this book and these words would not exist without the lifetime of moments we shared in such a short amount of time.

Lastly, Thank you to my online community at TikTok & Instagram. I could write "thank you" a million times and still not express what you mean to me. You all have given me the courage to create in a way I never thought possible. This book is for you. Thank you.

Made in United States
Orlando, FL
08 April 2023

31877144R00049